# Echoes Of A Heart Unspoken

Echoes of My Life

Subharti Sengupta

BookLeaf Publishing

India | USA | UK

Made with ❤ on the BookLeaf Publishing Platform

www.bookleafpub.in

www.bookleafpub.com

# Dedication

To those people who like to express themselves in words
and find solace for their emotions.

# Preface

*"What matters in life is not what happens to you but what you remember and how you remember it."*
— Gabriel García Márquez

Life has a way of teaching us through experiences —
sometimes gently, often painfully. This book is a
collection of poems shaped by my own journey through
love, heartbreak, healing, and self-belief. It is a reflection
of my day-to-day struggles, the emotions I've carried,
and the strength I've found in expressing them through
words.

I chose to write this book not just for myself, but for
anyone who has ever felt overwhelmed by their feelings,
who has loved deeply, or who has experienced loss in
any form. I wanted to reach out to those who, like me,
search for clarity, comfort, and connection in moments
of silence and stillness.

Each poem in this book is a piece of my story — raw,
honest, and deeply personal. They are expressions of
what it means to keep going, to cope, and to grow. I hope
these words remind you that your emotions are valid,
your story matters, and that writing can be a powerful
way to heal.

To the readers who pick up this book: may you find
pieces of yourself in these pages, and may they

encourage you to keep believing in your own strength.

— Subharti Sengupta

# Acknowledgements

This book is a reflection of my journey, and there are many people to thank for guiding and shaping me along the way.

To my family, whose unwavering love and support have been the foundation of my strength. You have been my constant through every challenge and triumph, and I am forever grateful for your presence in my life.

To my friends, who have been my companions in joy and sorrow, thank you for your encouragement, laughter, and honest conversations that have made this journey both meaningful and memorable.

To my mentors, whose wisdom and guidance have helped me see beyond myself. Your belief in me has given me the courage to push forward when the road seemed unclear.

And to the many people who have entered my life, whether for a brief moment or a lasting presence. You may not know it, but your actions, words, or simply your being, have taught me invaluable lessons. You have helped me grow, heal, and understand myself in ways words cannot fully express.

Thank you, all of you, for helping me find my voice.

# 1. The Stars That Spoke

I wish we hadn't met in the month of June,

Life would have been real but not a looney tune,

I wish we hadn't met when the moon was full,

I would have been happy like a child returning home
from school,

I wish our stars didn't know how to talk, Life would have
been so different but not a lonely walk....

# 2. She May Not Be Your First

She may not be your first or last,
Nor the only love that's held you fast.
She's loved before, may love again,
Yet loves you now—so why pretend?

She isn't perfect—nor are you,
And flawless love is far too few.
But if she makes you laugh and dream,
And shares her soul in moonlight's gleam...

Then hold her close, don't let her go,
Give her the love that she should know.
She may not think of you all day,
But gives her heart in her own way.

So guard it well—don't let it break,
Don't shape her soul for your own sake.
Just smile when she brings you light and cheer,
And miss her most when she's not near.

# 3. Silent Murmurs

Lost in the hush of time, I sit and gaze,
A life rewritten in shadowed haze.
If only my choices had steered me right,
If only I'd dared in the absence of light.
A piece of me lingers where echoes remain,
Wishing the past had been softer, less vain.
If fate had been kind, if the winds had been mild,
Perhaps I'd have walked like a carefree child.
The one desire that slipped through my hands,
Would it have shattered or let me stand?
Yet one truth lingers, deep and pure,
I loved you with a heart so sure.
But where you once dwelled, there's only ache—
A wound that even time may never remake.

# 4. My Beloved Wife

You are more special than words can convey,
More cherished than my actions display.
My soul mate, my lover, my guiding light,
You are my everything, my heart's delight.

Your radiant smile, your captivating eyes,
The warmth of your heart, your tender cries.
I promise to love you beyond this life,
Through eternity, beyond all strife.

My dearest friend, the essence of my life,
My beacon of hope, my beloved wife.
Your strength upholds me, your shoulder consoles,
For you, I'd traverse any length, any shoal.

You are my anchor, steadfast and true,
The one I rely on, my refuge in view.
Having you now feels like a dream,
Yet time with you is too fleeting, it seems.

The present is precious, yet not enough,
Forever with you wouldn't be too much.
Without you, I'd be lost, unsure what to do,
For you are my compass, my north star, my truth.

More than a friend, more than a wife,
You are my forever, the love of my life.
Yet even forever feels too brief,
For the journey I envision with you, my sweet.

In heaven, there's a place reserved for you,
I pray there's room beside you for me too.
Your soul is beautiful, a treasure to behold,
I vow to cherish you, forever to hold.

Together, always, through life's endeavor,
I pray we remain, now and forever.

# 5. Only Once

Only once in your life, I truly believe,
You meet someone who makes your world breathe.
They listen like no one ever has before,
Hungry for truths, for dreams, for more.

You speak of hopes and faded schemes,
Of broken paths and forgotten dreams.
Yet in their eyes, no judgment lies—
Just love that hears and never denies.

When joy arrives, they're the first you call,
To laugh with you, to share it all.
And when the tears begin to fall,
They hold you close and feel it all.

They never wound with careless word,
But lift you up with kindness heard.
In their presence, calmness grows,
Like gentle rain or falling snow.

You're free to be your truest self,
No masks, no games, no need for stealth.
Each shared note, each song, each glance—
Becomes a sacred, sweet romance.

Old memories rise, like winds through trees,
Childhood laughter, moments free.
Colors bloom in deeper hue,
As if the world's been born anew.

Their voice, a balm in darkest hour,
Their presence, quiet, steady power.
No need to speak, just sit, just stay—
And somehow all drifts far away.

Their world becomes a part of you,
And suddenly, the sky is blue.
A breeze, a storm, a cloud above,
All whisper softly of their love.

You open your heart, though it may break,
For joy that's real is worth the ache.
You find in love both strength and fear—
And yet, you're glad to have them near.

Perhaps a soul mate, perhaps a friend,

A light that guides you to the end.
Life feels brighter, bold and new—
All because they walk with you.

# 6. Fly Away With You

There are times in life, we stop and stare,
Look back slow, with a silent care.
And when I turned, what did I see?
That love is all—it's all for me.

It's all we chase, it's all we know,
A fire that sets our souls aglow.
And in your eyes, that fire burns—
A gaze for which my own heart yearns.

Your hair flows wild in the breeze,
A sight that brings my heart to ease.
In that moment, I feel so high—
Like I could reach and touch the sky.

I need that love, I need it true,
Without it, I don't know what to do.
For love, it lifts, it makes me free,
Just like a kite above the sea.

And when our eyes begin to meet,
My heart forgets to keep its beat.
It dares to break, it dares to fly,
To leave the ground, to touch the sky.

Fly away, fly away—just us two,
Fly away, fly away—with you.
No more chains, no skies too blue,
I only want to fly—with you.

# 7. If Only You Can See

If only you can see my eyes now
you will read all the untold words
If only you can see through them
you will understand that for me you are the world

If only you can see the smile on my face
when i receive your email, message or phone call
you will know that you have captured me all

If only you can see what happens to me the moment we
meet
If only you can feel how fast my heart beat
you will know that you are the only one who makes me
feel complete

# 8. My Pen

Hugging my soft pillow
As I gather my lost shattered thoughts
I reach for my pen
My best friend. My old fellow

How much I turn to you, my pen?
Cause you're the only one
who knows me deeply from within
You're always there for me
through thick & thin!

And when I was only ten
you were patient with my silly childish dreams
Like dreaming of being a prince in a legend!
Or becoming a handsome King!

You were patient enough with my weird stupid
questions
Like why the sky is blue & not green?
And when I turned 18

Still I'm holding on to you
I'm still so keen
For you're the truest friend I've ever seen!

You always listen & listen & listen
When no one else seems to be there
You're always there
When all other people just don't care
And my most special thoughts
with me you share

Even the hard feelings
You make me spit it all out of my chest
You take that burden
And make me always relax & rest

I turn to you
When I'm so weak
For you're the only one who understands me
When I really feel like I can't speak

You're the only one
Who could read my speechless mind
I turn to you
When all the world is against me and not on my side
You know my every secret
For with you there is nothing to hide

Cause I know my secrets you won't reveal
You put my feelings into words
For you know what I exactly feel

You help me to be what I want
You always encourage me
You never tell me ' YOU CAN'T '

I dreamed to be a poet
And on this moment
I want to thank you
For you're the one
Who let me notice my talent!

# 9. Alone

I was all alone
Wanted to live all by my own
I was afraid.. maybe even scared
Never wanted my life to be shared

I was full of fear
Until you appear
Comforting me.. telling me
You will always be around
You will always be near

I was so lonely
Until that special day
When you promised that you will love me only

I thought it was another lie
A story that will fade and die
And soon you will say goodbye

I didn't want to start

For I didn't want to see an un-happy end
I didn't want a broken heart
For this time I really won't know how it would be mend?

You never gave up
You just shower me with your endless care
And your perfect love that I could not compare
You gave me confidence.. You pushed me to dare

Dare to love once more
To have something precious in my life to live for
To open my heart.. To open my eyes
To open the passion's door

To give myself and my heart another chance
To feel the real romance

I need no wasted years
I need no un-stopped tears
I don't want to feel so blue
I just want a serious relation
One to be so true

I wantd to love but still be free
I wanted someone to love me
For what I am and not what I will be

Someone to love me as I am
And never expect me to change
Someone who will set me free
Like a bird flying out of its cage

You touched me deep inside
You're so tender.. You're so kind
You're someone I longed to find

You take my hands
You always try to understand
You make me feel so complete
You're simply so sweet!

I'm so happy that finally
I have found love that is so pure and divine!
I really hope that we will never be apart
I will always be yours just like you will always be mine!
You are my sweetest valentine!

I Love you.. I really do
I don't know
Where or when or how? !
I have no clue!

I Just love you.. Only you
I will always love you

Until forever
I will cherish you!

# 10. The Laugh She Borrows

She giggles like she gets it—
My joke, a tangled thread,
She nods as if it's crystal clear,
Though nothing's really said.

Her eyes, they hold a sparkle,
A secret she won't share,
Like she's in on life's great mystery,
With ribbons in her hair.

That laugh—it's part pretend, I know,
But pure and true in part,
It wraps around my silly words
And melts my very heart.

She plays along so perfectly,
As if to let me win,
The kind of grace that only grows
From laughter deep within.

So I keep on with my stories,
My riddles, jokes, and lore,
Because her "knowing" giggle
Is the sound I treasure more.

# 11. My Sister, My Strength

You stood beside me quietly,
No need for grand display,
Just knowing you were always there
Could chase my fears away.

A voice that calms the thunder,
A hug that feels like truth,
You've been my steady anchor
Since the wild days of our youth.

Through storms I didn't speak of,
And battles none could see,
You offered strength in silence—
You simply let me be.

You never asked for credit,
No medals on your chest,
But in the story of my life,
You've always been the best.

When I forget my power,
You lend me some of yours,
With words that build me quietly
And love that reassures.

So here's to you, my sister—
My compass, heart, and friend,
A bond that life keeps proving
Will never break or bend.

# 12. Coffee with a Known Stranger

The door swings wide, you step inside,
Not as the storm, but as the tide.
Calm, familiar, yet somehow new —
A past reshaped, a clearer view.

We sit, and time begins to pour
Like cream into the coffee's core.
The bitterness we once had steeped
Now softened into something sweet.

You speak — not of the wounds we bore,
But how we've grown, and learned, and more.
I see it there behind your eyes:
Not lost love, but love revised.

A joke, a spark, a quiet grin,
As if the light just let us in.
The air is warmer, hearts less guarded,
Two stories paused, and now restarted.

No rush to name it, no demand —
Just fingers brushing, hand to hand.
And maybe, in this café's glow,
A stranger's heart I've come to know.

Not as an echo, or a ghost —
But something real I missed the most.
A second chance, both brave and tender,
Over coffee... with a known stranger.

# 13. Echoes of Her Smile

Love blossomed, genuine and true,
Not a fleeting fancy, but a bond we grew.
She'd wait, fifteen minutes, maybe more,
Greeting me sweetly, as I reached the door.

Her dress, a vision, etched in my mind,
Rickshaw rides with her, leaving worries behind.
Her smile, like lavender, fresh and bright,
Chased away my fatigue, filled me with light.

In her embrace, my soul found rest,
A soothing balm upon my chest.
Her stories, endless, held me near,
Each word a melody I longed to hear.

Her lips, like rivers, shifting course,
Flowing with grace, a natural force.
Her hand in mine, a touch so divine,
Assuring me she'd always be mine.

Unspoken words, yet I could see,
Our bond was deepening, endlessly.
In every gesture, every glance,
Love did happen—not by chance.

# 14. Gazing out the window

Gazing out the window, streetlights illuminate the road below.
Yet, within me, shadows loom, yearning for a golden glow.
I know it's challenging to break free,
When shackled by sorrow, still longing to swing passionately.

If you're reading this, cherish the life you live,
For the essence lies in the fight, the will to persist.
Through the pane, I observe a boy dancing in the rain, believing he's unbound,
Yet an unseen darkness encircles him, preventing him from being found.

The streetlights fade from view,
It's consuming him—does he have a clue?
I ache witnessing his solitary plight,
But he's a loner; perhaps it's his chosen fight

Looking out, I realize this truth profound:
In joyous times, companions abound,
But in moments steeped in sadness and strife,
It's often just me, facing the night.

# 15. The Voice of Cracked

# Thunder

He had the voice of cracked thunder,
Rumbling deep, a storm's reminder,
A sound that echoed through the night,
A power hidden in plain sight.

It shook the walls, but not with fear,
A steady force that drew me near,
With every word, a truth so clear,
A quiet strength that could not disappear.

His laugh, like rain on parched ground,
His silence, the calm before it found
The storm again, where words could play,
And guide me through the darkest day.

I knew that voice, though rough and worn,
Had shaped the man that I'd been born
To know, to love, to rise, to stand,
With the thunder still held in my hand.

For in that voice, I'd always hear
The wisdom of a life so dear,
A thunderclap that echoes still,
A father's love, unbroken, real.

# 16. Her Smile

Her smile was like the gentlest breeze,
A soothing touch among life's seas.
Her laughter, like a songbird's call,
Bringing joy and warmth to all.

Her eyes, like glittering pearls, remain embedded in my
heart,
Reflecting love in every part.
Her voice, a melody so sweet,
A lullaby, my soul's retreat.

Her hands, like paintbrushes, paint vibrancy on the
dullest of days,
Crafting dreams in hues ablaze.
Her embrace, a sheltering tree,
A haven for my heart to be.

Her spirit, fierce as lightning's spark,
Guiding me through paths once dark.
Her love, a beacon shining true,

A constant light in all I do.

Mother, you're my heart's refrain,
A symphony of joy and pain.
Through every storm and gentle breeze,
Your love remains, my soul's ease

# 17. My Little Light

In your laughter lives the morning,
Bright as sunshine through the rain,
Every smile a gentle promise
That joy will always reign.

Tiny hands that hold my heart,
Eyes like stars that light the skies,
You teach me love without a word,
Just being you is wise.

The world is wide, your dreams are wide,
And you will chase them all,
I'll cheer for every mountain climbed,
Catch you if you fall.

Your voice, a song of innocence,
Your steps, a dance of grace,
And every day, I see anew
The wonder in your face.

You are my hope, my sweetest part,
The calm within the wild—
Forever proud, forever blessed
To call you my dear child.

# 18. My Shield in the Hallways

You weren't just a sister—
You were fire wrapped in grace,
Charging through the schoolyard
Like a storm in second place.

When words were sharp as arrows,
And I was shrinking small,
You stood between me and the world,
Refusing I should fall.

You didn't need permission,
You didn't wait or pause,
You fought the battles I ignored—
Just because you saw the cause.

I'd watch you face the loudest ones
With courage in your stare,
And somehow, in your silence,
I knew that you were there.

Now years have passed and life has grown
In gentler, brighter ways,
But still, I feel your warrior soul
Beside me in my days.

You're still the strength I lean on,
The calm when I'm not sure—
My sister, my defender,
My constant, quiet cure.

# 19. A Half Healed Heart

We sit across, the table small,
Two porcelain cups, the silence tall.
Steam curls like thoughts we never said,
The weight of years between us spread.

Your eyes, still mapped in memory's glow,
Familiar tides I used to know.
Yet now they drift on stranger seas,
With stories whispered by the breeze.

We stir the sugar, sip the past,
In echoes of a love that couldn't last.
Our words are kind, but fenced and few,
Like postcards from a place we knew.

Your laugh, a faded photograph,
I smile — a mask, a broken half.
Still, here we are, in borrowed grace,
Two ghosts who share the same old space.

# 20. We Meet Again

We meet again — not quite the same,
Years softened us, and dulled the blame.
The café hums, a gentle thread,
Binding all the words unsaid.

Your smile is new, yet still familiar,
Like morning light through old cathedral.
Not who you were, nor who I knew,
But something kind, and somehow true.

We speak in ease, not chased by fire,
No ashes left, no lost desire.
Just stories shared with open hands,
Two souls that time could still remand.

No need to name what slipped away,
Some things are meant to change, not stay.
But in this brew, this quiet blend,
I find a stranger — and a friend.

# 21. The Mirror Crack'd

The mirror crack'd from side to side,
A whisper crept where silence died.
No hand had touched, no breath had stirred—
Yet through the glass, a voice was heard.
Its edges bled with silver flame,
Each crack a mouth that spoke my name.
The room grew still, the candles bowed,
The shadows thickened like a shroud.
I saw a figure not my own,
A face I wore, yet not alone.
Its eyes too deep, its smile too wide—
A stranger on the other side.
The wind began to keen and cry,
The clock forgot to mark the time.
A chill ran slow along my spine—
The mirror crack'd. The fault was mine.
It watches now from dusk till dawn,
That broken glass I gazed upon.
And every night, it hums the rhyme:
**"The curse is come, the crack is time."**

www.ingramcontent.com/pod-product-compliance
Lightning Source LLC
Chambersburg PA
CBHW070609160726
48003CB00005B/2185